This book belongs to:

_____

_____

For Thomas Sankara, African revolutionary, who knew that "women hold up the other half of the sky." And for my father, who was his friend.

A

For my father, the first African in my life—I wish he'd seen this book.

MF

• First US edition 2021 • First published by Walker Books Ltd. (UK) 2019 • Library of Congress Catalog Card Number pending • ISBN 978-1-5362-0537-4 • This book was typeset in Clarendon T and Gill Sans MT Schoolbook. The illustrations were done in mixed media.
Candlewick Press, 99 Dover Street, Somerville, Massachusetts 02144 • www.candlewick.com
Printed in Shenzhen, Guangdong, China • 22 23 24 25 26 CCP 10 9 8 7 6 5 4 3

Africa
AMAZING AFRICA

Atinuke

illustrated by
Mouni Feddag

CANDLEWICK PRESS

Contents

Central Africa ... 54

North Africa ... 66

Introduction

WRITING this book has been an adventure. I wanted to write it so that I could share the things I find exciting about Africa. But while I was working on it, I found out a zillion more really exciting things.

Did you know that the first human beings to walk this earth were African? They went on to populate the whole planet. So we are all from Africa originally!

Did you know that Africa is gigantic? It is as big as Europe, the United States, Mexico, India, and Japan all put together!

Did you know that no one can decide on the official number of African countries? This is because there are countries that are still unofficial. These are new countries that are struggling to become independent from other countries.

Did you know that in each African country, many different languages are spoken? This is because African countries are made up of lots of ancient African kingdoms. Those original kingdoms all had their own languages and customs, many of which still exist.

Africa is not one place. It has at least fifty-five different countries. And each country has many different cultures, different histories, and lots of different landscapes. African countries must be the most diverse on the planet!

Africa is hot, blinding deserts; wild, wet deltas; dark, dripping rain forests; white sandy beaches; flat, grassy savannas; cold, snowy mountains; black volcano islands; deep blue oceans; and more.

Africa is modern mega-cities with skyscrapers and highways.

Africa is ancient cities of clay with mosques and libraries. Africa is villages of huts with goats and chickens. Africa is shantytowns made out of cardboard and corrugated iron.

Africa is donkeys and diamonds, camels and Coca-Cola, lions and Lamborghinis, oil rigs and armies, football and ancient ruins, and more.

Africa is people: more than one billion people when I was writing this book, and more born every day. Almost half the people on the continent are young people—we have the youngest population on the planet!

Africa is also animals: thousands of incredible animals that are quickly becoming extinct. These animals were hunted for millennia by hunter-gatherers, who never threatened their existence. It is our modern lifestyles that are wiping them out.

Climate change is changing landscapes and cultures and the lifestyles and habitats of both animals and people. And so is the modern technological age.

Some African countries are incredibly modern, with cutting-edge hospitals and high-rise cities and fancy sports cars. Other countries are old-fashioned, with people herding camels and goats, and walking miles to collect water. Most, in fact, are both. Africa has always been a mixture of ancient traditions and innovations.

Africa was home to the first university in the world, more than two hundred years before Europe, and centers of learning thrived there more than a thousand years before that. It was in Africa that medicine, engineering, math, and astronomy were developed. African scholars knew that the earth was round and circled the sun centuries before European

scholars did. The first alphabets were invented in Africa, as well as the idea of counting in tens.

Today, inventors in African countries are making discoveries in medicine, robotics, software engineering, sustainable technology, banking, and more.

The world has a lot to thank Africa for!

This book is a celebration of Africa. But there is a lot of heartbreak as well. There is still slavery, still war, still hunger. We are one global village now, so to make Africa a better place, we have to make the whole world a better place. That means we can start right at home, wherever your home may be. One way to start is to buy things that are fair trade—this means they are made by people who are paid fairly for their work. This does make fair trade things more expensive, so we might not be able to buy as much as we are used to. But if we are willing to accept having less, then other people can have their fair share.

Africa is changing all the time: new countries are being created or swallowed up, old traditions are being lost and new ones developing. This book can only give an idea of what Africa is like in the moment that I am writing. So enjoy this book for what it is: a tiny glimpse into this wonderful continent.

I could not squeeze everything that I know and love about Africa into this book. There is room to say only two or three things about each country. But I hope this book will make you want to find out more about the most amazing continent on the planet!

Southern Africa

Angola, Botswana, Eswatini, Lesotho, Malawi, Mozambique, Namibia, South Africa, Zambia, and Zimbabwe

Southern Africa has long white beaches on the Indian and Atlantic Oceans, where people swim with whales and dolphins. Southern Africa has wide-open savannas, where giraffes, zebras, and rhinos roam and where hunters used to stalk them. Southern Africa has the oldest desert in the world, where, over millions of years, antelope, elephants, lions, and humans have learned to live. Southern Africa has modern cities, with big banks, cutting-edge hospitals, huge museums, and busy nightclubs. Most southern Africans have African ancestors, but some have ancestors from Europe or India. So southern Africa is home to Black people, white people, people of South Asian heritage, and people of mixed heritages.

Welcome to Southern Africa!

"Mauya!" (Shona), "Ngiyanemukela!" (Zulu),
"Welkom!" (Afrikaans), "Siyalemukela!" (Ndebele),
"Namkelekile!" (Xhosa), "Welcome!" (English)

Luanda

ANGOLA

ZAMBIA

MALAWI

Lake Malawi

MOZAMBIQUE

NAMIBIA

ZIMBABWE

BOTSWANA

SOUTH AFRICA

LESOTHO

ESWATINI

Indian Ocean

Atlantic Ocean

Angola

Angola's capital city, Luanda, is right on the beach, where skyscrapers overlook palm trees and big white yachts in the bay. In the offices, people are busy on their computers and cell phones, and in the streets, people are busy shouting their wares and honking their car horns. Outside the city is the rain forest: a place where the forest people tread silently with their spears and arrows; a place busy with butterflies, birds, monkeys, and lizards; a rain forest thick with trees that help our planet to breathe.

★ Basketball is very popular in Angola. Many of Angola's basketball players are signed by international teams.

* Angola's top exports are oil and diamonds.

⦿ The Brazilian martial art of capoeira probably came from Angola.

Botswana

Botswana is rich in diamonds, rich in cattle, and rich in wildlife. It is home to millionaires, home to cattle herders, and home to hunter-gatherers. The millionaires want to dig up the land and mine it for diamonds. The cattle-loving people want the land free of predators so their cattle can graze safely. To them, cattle are riches. The nomadic San people do not care about diamonds or cattle. They want the land to stay wild and free—just like them.

● Botswana's Tsodillo Hills, in the Kalahari Desert, are home to an extensive gallery of rock paintings and carvings by ancient nomadic peoples. They say it's on that very spot that the creation of the world began.

✱ Black rhinos were once extinct in Botswana, and white rhinos were so endangered that the people of a Botswanan village called Serowe made their land into a rhino sanctuary. White rhinos multiplied there, and one day a black rhino crossed the border from Zimbabwe into the sanctuary. Now there are four black rhinos living happily in Botswana!

Eswatini

The king of Eswatini is the last king in Africa, and everyone in his country has to do what he says—the army, the police, and even the newspapers. King Mswati III has lots of cars, lots of palaces, and lots of wives. He is very, very rich, but his people are very poor—and they are not all that happy about it!

★ Traditional houses in Eswatini are beautiful domes made of reeds and grasses.

◉ When there's a festival in Eswatini, people love to dress in bright traditional clothes, dance traditional dances, and sing traditional songs, all of which have not changed for hundreds of years. "The Land Is All for the King" is one of the songs!

Lesotho

Lesotho is one of the highest countries in the world, so it is called the "Kingdom in the Sky." Some places there can be reached only on foot or in small planes. It is snowy in winter and the skiing is great, but it's also very cold, so blankets are important. And people don't just sleep under blankets— they also wear them during the day. Now there are factories in Lesotho making clothes for international clothing companies, and people wear coats and jackets just as often as they wear their traditional blankets.

✱ There are fossilized dinosaur footprints in Lesotho that are more than 180 million years old!

● Lesotho sells electricity and water to its big neighbor, South Africa. A massive dam in the highlands funnels water to South Africa, and along the way, the water's flow generates electricity.

Malawi

Malawi is famous for its woven baskets and carved wooden masks. Now it's also known for its car fuel! Gasoline is expensive in Malawi, so to make cars cheaper to run, Malawians experimented with mixing ethanol (made from sugarcane or corn) with gasoline. Then they invented a kit that lets cars use ethanol alone. It's a very cheap way to get around.

✳ Malawi has some great young inventors and engineers. William Kamkwamba is one. When he was fourteen, he built a working windmill from old scrap metal after seeing a diagram in a library book.

★ Lake Malawi has more than 1,000 types of fish, and most of them are found only in the lake. These fish are so bright and beautiful that they are sold to pet shops all over the world for people to put in their tropical-fish tanks.

Mozambique

Football (known as soccer in the United States) is Mozambique's most popular sport. In cities, people crowd into football stadiums to watch their favorite teams play. In towns, children who are lucky enough practice on football pitches, and those who aren't play on the streets. In villages, children play on any bit of flat ground. And if there's not a real football, they'll make one out of rags or plastic bags or bark or rubber bands or anything, really!

✴ Peri-peri sauce comes from Mozambique, and the tiny chili peppers that grow there are called "piri-piri" in Swahili.

◉ Mozambique's national music is called marrabenta. It is changing fast as it mixes with hip-hop and rap, but some things stay the same—the rhythms still make people jump up and dance!

Namibia

In Namibia, there is a desert that runs right into the Atlantic Ocean, and there you'll find some of the biggest sand dunes on the planet. These pink and orange dunes are so enormous that people surf down them! The beaches are foggy because the hot desert air hits the cold Atlantic Ocean air and turns into fog. The fog prevents ships from seeing the jagged rocks along Namibia's coastline, so more than a thousand shipwrecks are scattered on those foggy beaches, along with the bones of whales and seals. No wonder it's called the "Skeleton Coast"!

★ In 2008, a shipwreck was discovered buried in the sand. It was a Portuguese ship that had disappeared in 1533 on its way to India. On board were gold coins and ivory worth more than $11.6 million.

✴ There is a salt desert in Namibia so white it can be seen from space. Another of Namibia's deserts used to sparkle not with salt but with diamonds, which you could collect just by running your hands through the sand!

South Africa

South Africa is called the "Rainbow Nation" because of its mix of Black people, white people, and people of South Asian descent. For many years, some of the white people, who decided they were better than anyone else, kept jobs, land, and education just for themselves. Other people, like Nelson Mandela, fought for everybody to be considered equal. Now that time is over, and South Africans are working together for peace. It is one of Africa's most modern countries: there are big cities like Johannesburg and Cape Town, with football stadiums, shopping malls, mansions, and poor neighborhoods, where all sorts of different people live and work and play.

⬤ Nelson Mandela was the first Black South African president. Before becoming president, he was kept in prison for twenty-seven years—and was told he would be freed only if he stopped fighting for equality for all South Africans. He always refused!

✱ There are lots of international car factories in South Africa, and the country has its own car companies, too, like Advanced Automotive Design, Bailey Cars, and Birkin Cars.

Zambia

Lots of people in Zambia carry things on their heads: baskets, buckets, and even sacks. It's much easier to carry heavy things with our strong neck muscles than with our skinny arms. Some people can do this without using their hands to hold things steady—even when they are running or riding motorbikes. It's beautiful and it's skillful, and it's done all over Africa.

● On the border between Zambia and Zimbabwe is the biggest waterfall on the planet. It is called Mosi-oa-Tunya, which means "the smoke that thunders," because when spray from the falling water hits the river below, it looks like smoke and can be seen from far away. In English, the falls are called "Victoria Falls."

★ Every year, 10 million or more fruit bats gather in Zambia. It's the biggest mammal migration on Earth!

Zimbabwe

Zimbabwe has incredible structures. It has modern cities full of skyscrapers and sculptures. It has the ancient ruined city of Great Zimbabwe. And most incredible of all, it has the balancing rocks in Matobo National Park. Some of these are rocks the size of cars, balanced on rocks the size of houses, balanced on rocks the size of football stadiums. Others are massive rocks the size of trucks, balanced on rocks the size of cars, balanced on rocks the size of shopping carts. These rocks have not wobbled for millions of years, so people not only climb them but they actually build houses in their shade!

● Great Zimbabwe was the capital city of an ancient kingdom. Some people have wondered whether precious metals and jewels mined in the kingdom were sold to the wise King Solomon. This would make Zimbabwe home to King Solomon's mines, which are mentioned in the Bible, the Torah, and the Quran.

East Africa

Comoros, Djibouti, Eritrea, Ethiopia, Kenya, Madagascar, Mauritius, Rwanda, Seychelles, Somalia, South Sudan, Sudan, Tanzania, and Uganda

East Africa is famous for its huge savannas where Africa's most popular animals live: elephants, lions, giraffes, zebras, and lots more. Out of those savannas rise Africa's tallest mountains, and there you will find its deepest lakes and most powerful waterfalls. East Africa is the part of Africa closest to Asia. For more than a thousand years, ships have come across the Indian Ocean from Asia, bringing tea, spices, silk, and gunpowder to swap for East African ebony, ivory, gold, salt, and labor. The Arab nations were also involved in the trade. The East African language of Swahili has lots of Asian and Arabic words from centuries of East African, Asian, and Arabic peoples doing business together. The Swahili city-states were thriving hundreds of years before Europeans knew that Africa (or even America) existed. Swahili is still the most common language in East Africa. And East Africa is still a melting pot of many different cultures, traditions, and religions.

Welcome to East Africa!

"Karibu!" (Swahili), "Inikwani dehina met'ahi!" (Amharic), "Baga nagaan dhufte!" (Oromo), "Soo dhowow" (Somali), "Ahlan wa sahlah!" (Arabic)

Mediterranean Sea

Suez Canal

Red Sea

SUDAN

ERITREA

DJIBOUTI
Djibouti

SOUTH
SUDAN

ETHIOPIA

SOMALIA

Indian
Ocean

UGANDA

KENYA
Nairobi

Lake
Victoria

RWANDA

SEYCHELLES

TANZANIA

COMOROS

MADAGASCAR

MAURITIUS

Indian
Ocean

Comoros

There are hundreds of mosques—Muslim houses of worship—on the islands of Comoros. Some are big and grand, while others are small and shabby. Most children go to Quranic schools, where they learn to read and write in flowing Arabic script and study the Quran, Islam's holy book. Beautiful scented flowers grow all over the islands. They are used to make sweet-smelling oils that are sold around the world to make perfumes. Some of the oils are even considered holy.

✴ Comoros is a group of four islands: Grande Comore, Mohéli, Anjouan, and Mayotte.

مرحبا!

"Marhaba!" (Arabic for "hello!")

◉ Islam is the biggest religion in Comoros. Laws in Comoros are mainly drawn from Islamic religious and common law.

Djibouti

For over 3,500 years, ships from Africa and Asia and Europe have stopped in Djibouti to trade. Even today the capital city is one of the busiest ports in the world, where container ships refuel and change cargo. Outside the city, the land is mostly desert, where nomads live. People say it is like the moon, with white salt lakes and cracked earth and tall rocky pillars that puff out steam.

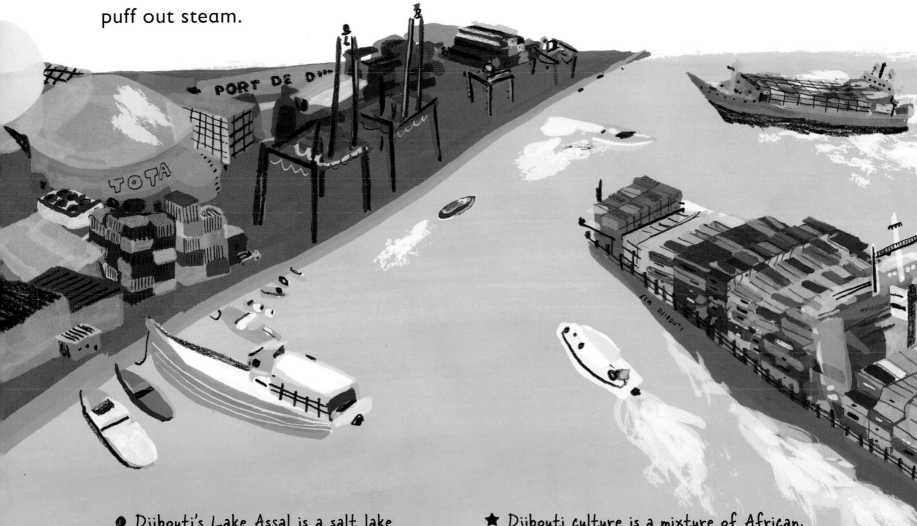

● Djibouti's Lake Assal is a salt lake and the lowest place on the African continent: 500 feet (155 meters) below sea level.

★ Djibouti culture is a mixture of African, French, Arabic, and other influences. Even the food is a mixture. Sambusas, a popular Djiboutian snack, are much like Indian samosas.

Eritrea

Eritrea is home to many nomadic peoples who live in tents made of woven mats that let in cool breezes. Eritrea's nomads are constantly on the move, chasing the rains that fill drinking wells and water the grass that their goats, camels, and cattle need to thrive. Nomads depend on their herds for meat and milk, as the land is too dry to grow food. The nomadic way of life is the oldest human lifestyle. But nomads are modern now, too—some use GPS and cell phone apps to check where the rain and the best grass are.

---

* In Eritrea's war of independence (1961-1991), more than a third of the army were women.

☉ There are almost six hundred species of bright and beautiful birds in Eritrea. It's on a migration route, so many of the species can be seen in Europe as well.

Ethiopia

Ethiopia was one of the first Christian countries in the world—maybe *the* first! In Christianity's early days, Christians were often attacked for their beliefs, so many churches in Ethiopia were built in safe places in the high mountains—places that were hard to get to. Some of the churches are carved into underground rocks, and others built so high up in cliffs that you have to climb to reach them. Inside, they are painted with huge, beautiful, brightly colored murals of Christian saints, kings, apostles, and angels.

⦿ In the 1800s, European countries seized all of Africa except Ethiopia. Ethiopia's independence inspired other African countries when they began to fight to be free of European rule.

⦿ Ethiopia also inspired Rastafarianism, a religion practiced in Jamaica that takes its name from Ethiopia's last emperor, Ras Tafari.

✱ It is thought that coffee first came from Ethiopia—and from there, the habit of drinking it spread all over the world.

Kenya

Kenya is famous for its lions, elephants, giraffes, zebras, rhinoceroses, and hippopotamuses. But its city life is as wild and wonderful as its wildlife. In the crowded streets of the capital, Nairobi, people of African, Indian, Chinese, Arabic, and European descent hustle and bustle in and out of shopping malls, jumping on and off the colorful buses, chatting into their phones—or doing their online banking!

🌐 Kenya is named after its tallest mountain, Mount Kenya. The name is thought to mean "God's Resting Place."

✿ Nairobi is right on the edge of Nairobi National Park. Only a powerful electric fence keeps the animals from roaming the city streets. The giraffes in the park have a good view of the skyscrapers downtown. And in the city, you really can see giraffes on the horizon!

Madagascar

Madagascar is an island that broke away from Africa and into the Indian Ocean 88 million years ago. There are 200,000 species of animals there, and about 80 percent of them cannot be found anywhere else on the planet. There are chameleons as big as cats, geckos that look like dead leaves, and frogs the color of tomatoes!

* There were no people on Madagascar when the island broke away. The first people to arrive came from Indonesia and Malaysia. Even now, the food, languages, and customs of Madagascar are mostly Southeast Asian.

* Humpback whales come near the coast of Madagascar to breed. It is one of the best places in the world for watching them jump and listening to them sing.

Mauritius

Mauritius is the only African country where Hinduism is the main religion. Around half of all Mauritians are Hindu; the others are mainly Christian or Muslim. Hinduism is an Indian religion; Hindus worship lots of different gods in beautiful golden temples. Mauritian money is called the rupee, just as it is in India. This is because most people in Mauritius are descended from Indian immigrants. The rest are from Africa, China, or Europe. And they are all immigrants, too, because nobody lived on the island at all until 1683!

● There were no predators on Mauritius until humans came. With no predators to worry about, many birds evolved to be large and flightless. One species was called the dodo. Dodos are now extinct—they were too easily caught by the hungry sailors who discovered the island.

★ There is a cyber city on the island, where people work in high-tech facilities.

✳ Ameenah Gurib became the first woman president of Mauritius in 2015. She is not only a politician. She is also a world-famous biologist.

Rwanda

The name Rwanda means "Land of a Thousand Hills." It is a tiny country high up in the mountains that has almost no flat places. The roads go either up, up, up . . . or down, down, down. The hills and mountains of Rwanda are farmed to grow tea and coffee that are sold all over the world. It's hard to grow things on steep slopes, so the farmers cut flat fields into the mountains that look like giant green curving steps.

✤ Some mountains are still covered with wild forests, where rare mountain gorillas thrive. Adult male gorillas are over 6 feet (2 meters) tall, with an arm span of 8 feet (2.4 meters)! They know how to open poachers' traps to rescue their loved ones and have been known to care for motherless gorilla babies.

Seychelles

Seychelles is a country made up of 115 islands! They're all full of beautiful birds, astonishing animals, and peculiar plants: rare black parrots and giant tortoises, trees with fruit like jellyfish, and the biggest nuts in the world! Luckily, Seychelles has the smallest population in Africa, so there is plenty of room for the birds, animals, and plants. In fact, more than half of the islands have been made into nature reserves.

● Creole is an official language in Seychelles. Creole is a language made up of other languages. It's such a mix that it's incomprehensible to speakers of the original languages.

Somalia

Somali people love poetry. Once, they recited poetry as they herded their flocks on land and fished on the ocean. But war, drought, and famine came. And big foreign fishing trawlers that scooped up all the fish. Now some of those herders and fishermen make a living as pirates, chasing huge container ships in their little speedboats. But Somali poets are their nation's true heroes, and they are still creating poetry.

★ Mo Farah, a British distance runner and one of the greatest athletes the world has ever known, was born in Somalia to Somali parents and lived there until he was eight. He is famous for winning double gold medals—twice!

✸ Somali people live all over the world now; many are refugees.

South Sudan

South Sudan is a very traditional country, where the Dinka and Nuer people grow their own food and herd fierce long-horned cattle. Many children learn at home instead of going to school. Girls learn how to grow food, and boys learn how to look after the cattle. Boys are given a young bull of their own. The boys and their bulls grow up together and are even called by the same name.

● South Sudan has the biggest savanna in Africa. These unfenced grasslands go on for thousands of miles, and huge herds of wild animals live there.

✳ In South Sudan, a herd of cattle is like money in the bank. The more cattle you have, the more important you feel. And if you need cash, you can sell a cow—like using your debit card!

Sudan

Sudan is one of the hottest and driest countries in the world. As camels can go months without drinking, they used to be the most popular mode of transport in Sudan before cars were invented. There are still camel markets everywhere, and camel races, which are loud and colorful and fun. Watch out, though—grumpy camels spit down on people from their great height, and their burps and farts can go on for two minutes! But the people in Sudan are some of the friendliest in the world.

★ There are more pyramids in Sudan than there are in Egypt. Both countries were once part of the ancient Kush kingdom, ruled from Sudan by the Nubian people. The Nubians were incredible archers and invented alphabetic writing.

✱ The Blue Nile River and the White Nile River meet in Sudan. If you stand on the bridge where they meet, you can see their two different colors flowing side by side.

33

Tanzania

Tanzania is a country in two parts: the mainland of Tanganyika and the island of Zanzibar. The mainland is famous for the millions of animals that travel up its enormous Serengeti savanna each year, following the rain that ripens the grass. They have to cross rivers full of hungry crocodiles lying in wait—so not all of them make it! Zanzibar is famous for its busy markets, which are rich with the scents of spices and the voices of merchants from all around the world.

✳ Thousands of years ago, sailors from Indonesia and India brought nutmeg, cloves, vanilla, and cinnamon to Zanzibar. The plants grow there still.

✳ When Tanganyika and Zanzibar became one country, a new word was created: Tanzania.

◉ Africa's tallest mountain, snowcapped Mount Kilimanjaro, rises out of the Serengeti.

Uganda

Trucks, buses, taxis, and matatu minibuses are everywhere in Uganda. Matatu drivers don't set off until the bus is overflowing, and they stop to drop passengers off whenever one shouts "Stop!" Old people squash together on seats with their shopping bags, and young people hang out windows clutching their college books and laughing into their phones. Chickens and goats are squeezed in, too, and roof racks groan under bags and packages and huge bunches of bananas.

@ Lake Nyanza is the biggest tropical lake in the world: 45 percent of it is in Uganda, 6 percent is in Kenya, and 49 percent is in Tanzania. It is the size of a small country. The first European who saw it was so amazed, he named it after the most awesome person he knew: Queen Victoria!

❀ Dividing Uganda and Democratic Republic of the Congo are the beautiful, snowcapped, glacial Ruwenzori Mountains, also called the "Mountains of the Moon."

West Africa

Benin, Burkina Faso, Cabo Verde, Côte d'Ivoire, The Gambia, Ghana, Guinea, Guinea-Bissau, Liberia, Mali, Niger, Nigeria, Senegal, Sierra Leone, and **Togo**

---- ✳ ----

In the north of West Africa lies the Sahara. In the south are the windy beaches of the Atlantic Ocean. In between is the starry Sahel, where the desert meets the grassy savannas; the savannas merge into dark rain forests, which melt into the wet mangrove swamps. The busy, crowded cities rock to the rhythms of highlife and hip-hop, because whether they are blue-eyed desert nomads or dark Black city dwellers, West Africans love music. Wherever you go, men wear long, flowing embroidered robes over loose baggy trousers—when they are not wearing blue jeans. Once, camels carried West African gold across the Sahara to the Middle East, and some of the world's first universities were founded in the region. Now West African companies sell diamonds and oil, and highly educated West African doctors, lawyers, and engineers work all over the world.

Welcome to West Africa!

"EKaBO!" (Yoruba), "Sannu da zuwa!" (Hausa), "Nnoo!" (Igbo), "How far?" (Pidgin), "Kusheh-o" (Krio), "Bienvenue!" (French), "Akwaaba" (Twi), "Dalal ak diam!" (Wolof), "Woezor!" (Ewe), "I ni sogoma!" (Bambara), "Welcome!" (English)

African Religions

Christianity and Islam are the most popular organized religions in Africa, but there are traditional religions, too. These religions teach that everything in the world has a soul—even trees, even rocks, even rivers, even storms! This is the oldest religious belief in the world and one that all our ancestors shared. Traditional religions have many gods (some kind and some cruel) all ruled by one top god.

Christianity and Islam arrived in Africa as soon as they began. Disciples of Jesus (in the first century) and Muhammad (in the seventh century) came to Africa to spread their religions. Some of the oldest mosques in the world are in North Africa. Some of the oldest churches in the world are in East Africa. And some of the oldest synagogues in the world are in Africa, too.

Christian and Muslim soldiers tried to destroy the traditional religions, but they didn't succeed. Most Africans are now either Christian or Muslim, but they still honor their traditional gods with drumming, dancing, and gifts.

Benin

The traditional religion Vodun is one of Benin's official religions. It is celebrated with festivals of drumming and dancing, where the ancestors and the traditional gods are worshipped. Vodun was taken to the Americas by enslaved Africans hundreds of years ago and is one of Haiti's official religions.

◉ Benin was once part of the kingdom of Dahomey, which began in the 1600s and lasted about three hundred years. The kingdom had a powerful army, and its women soldiers were considered the best and bravest of all. Seh-Dong-Hong-Beh was a commander when she was only a teenager.

✳ The wonderful Pendjari National Park in Benin is one of the very few places where West African lions still roam free.

Burkina Faso

The name Burkina Faso means "Land of the Honest People." It had a great president, Thomas Sankara, who said, "We must choose either champagne for a few or safe drinking water for all." So you won't see as many fancy buildings and fancy cars in Burkina Faso as you will in the rest of West Africa. Here bikes are the favorite way to get around—no matter what you're carrying or how many of you there are!

★ Burkina Faso has lots of big shady shea trees and sells shea butter all over the world to make creams and lotions to soften skin and hair.

◉ Caterpillars are a popular food in Burkina Faso. The yummiest are shea caterpillars, which eat only the leaves of shea trees.

Cabo Verde

Around 20 million years ago, volcanoes started erupting in the Atlantic Ocean. When the volcanoes cooled down after 12 million years, the molten lava hardened into an archipelago of islands off the coast of West Africa now called Cabo Verde. Sea levels around the world are rising because of climate change, and one day the beautiful islands of Cabo Verde may disappear back under the sea.

✻ More people from Cabo Verde live abroad in foreign countries than actually live in Cabo Verde! This is because life can be hard and scary there. Volcanoes still erupt from time to time, jobs are hard to find, and sometimes the fresh water runs out.

Côte d'Ivoire

The name Côte d'Ivoire means "Ivory Coast." The name comes from the huge ivory tusks of the elephants that once lived there. These big, beautiful elephants roamed with their families, making sure their babies always walked safely in the middle of the herd. When foreigners first arrived in Côte d'Ivoire, they killed as many of the elephants as they could and sold their tusks. Now more elephants are dying as their rain forest homes are destroyed, and many more are still being poached. The big, loving West African forest elephants are now nearly extinct.

✻ Elephants grieve when they lose a family member, covering their bodies with leaves and visiting their graves for years and years afterward.

★ Côte d'Ivoire is the biggest exporter of cocoa beans in the world! Maybe your favorite chocolate bar is made from cocoa that grew there.

The Gambia

This tiny country runs along the banks of the River Gambia. And there live not only Gambian people but also Gambian birds—nearly six hundred different kinds. There are herons, pelicans, and flamingos; guinea fowl, falcons, and hoopoes; paradise fly-catchers, sunbirds, and drongos. And tiny, tiny honeyguides, which communicate with humans.

◉ The Gambia is the smallest country on mainland Africa. It is no more than 30 miles (50 kilometers) wide in most places.

★ The Gambia has more than ninety stone circles that are nearly 2,000 years old. They are believed to be built around the burial mounds of ancient kings and chiefs.

✳ Honeyguides spend their lives looking for honey. When they spot a beehive they quickly fly to a person and whistle and whistle, calling for them to come and break open the hive. People are quick to follow because everyone loves honey!

Ghana

Ghana has the biggest market in the whole of West Africa. Thousands and thousands of people jostle their way through the walkways, buying and selling clothes and fruit, computers and cloth, dried fish and shoes, and everything else under the hot, hot sun. There are no set prices in an African market—the trader tells you what they want you to pay, and it's up to you to argue the price down. This is called haggling—it's fast and furious and full of jokes!

● Kente is the name of special Ghanaian cloth woven with silk and cotton. Once, only members of the royal family of the Ashante kingdom were allowed to wear it. Now anyone who's rich enough to buy it can wear it.

✶ Kejetia Market has around 10,000 stalls, and more than 44,000 people work there. It covers 30 acres (12 hectares)—that is as big as a small town.

Guinea

Like people in many parts of Africa, people in Guinea love buying bright and beautiful cloth in the markets. There are so many colors and patterns to choose from. There is cloth printed with animals, cloth printed with flowers, and cloth printed with famous presidents, expensive cars, and cell phones! People make the cloth into fabulous new outfits for work and for weddings.

* The most popular cloth in Guinea is batik. Batik dyeing was invented in Indonesia. European travelers learned it there and brought the technique with them to Africa. Batik cloth is made all over the continent now.

Guinea-Bissau

Babies are tied onto their mothers' backs with cloth everywhere in Guinea-Bissau. Tiny little newborn babies, small babies sucking their thumbs, big babies wearing shoes—all are carried by Mama when she is cooking or carrying water or riding to the bank on the back of a motorbike taxi. And if Mama is resting or in the office—well, there is always a sibling or a cousin to strap Baby onto.

★ Along the coast of Guinea-Bissau are mangrove swamps—tropical places where the sea turns rivers salty. Mangrove trees are the only trees in the world that can grow on salty, muddy riverbanks.

✳ Off the coast is a group of eighty-eight beautiful islands called Bijagós—each one is like an island paradise, where cute little pygmy hippopotamuses live!

Liberia

Liberia is Africa's oldest democratic nation and was never conquered by Europeans. It was established by African Americans nearly two hundred years ago. For centuries, African people had been kidnapped by Europeans and forced to work in America, Europe, and the Caribbean in slavery. Years later a group returned to Africa and started their own country—Liberia, whose name means "Land of Freedom."

● Liberia has a special handshake: the finger-snap handshake. Look for it online!

✴ In 1995, Liberian George Weah was named African, European, and World Football Player of the Year—the first footballer to ever achieve this. In 2018, he became president of Liberia.

Mali

Mali is a desert country—one of the hottest in the world. People wear billowing tunics and turbans to protect their skin from the scorching sun. Buildings are built with thick clay bricks to keep them cool and tiny windows to keep out the sun. There are whole cities made of clay in Mali—clay houses, clay mosques, clay shops, and clay schools.

● Mali was the center of one of the great African kingdoms—the kingdom of Mali, which stretched all the way to Lake Chad in the east and to the Atlantic Ocean in the south. It was more advanced than Europe at the time and one of the largest kingdoms in the world.

★ For centuries, the city of Timbuktu was an important place of learning where Islam, medicine, surgery, science, math, astronomy, literature, and art were studied. Its libraries still hold some of the world's most ancient manuscripts.

Niger

In Niger, most people are farmers or cattle herders. The farmers live in the wet south, where there is enough rain to grow crops. The herders roam the dry north, where there is just enough grass to feed their goats and cattle and camels. Every year in the dry season when the grass dries up, the herders travel south. The farmers have harvested their crops by then, and the herds can graze the stubble in the fields. By the time they leave, the fields are fertilized with cattle poop—and both farmers and herders are happy!

* Rock art in the desert in Niger shows the amazing animals that lived in the Sahara when it was a green savanna, rich in life—there are pictures of hippos and crocodiles, and life-size carvings of giraffes. Now it is so hot in the Sahara that rain often evaporates before it hits the ground!

* Horse racing, camel racing, traditional wrestling, and boxing are the most popular sports in Niger.

Nigeria

The city of Lagos in Nigeria is the biggest, busiest city in the whole of Africa. There are so many millions of cars that often the traffic is completely jammed for hours. So the quickest way to get around the city is on motorbike taxis. They can weave between cars, whether the cars are stuck or speeding. They're so dangerous, they've been banned on some roads, but not everyone in Lagos obeys the rules.

◉ Nigeria has the biggest population in Africa and the biggest economy. One in four Africans is Nigerian.

✸ The Hausa cities of Kano and Katsina in northern Nigeria are around 1,000 years old.

★ Nigeria has the third-largest film industry after Hollywood and Bollywood—"Nollywood"!

Senegal

In Senegal, music is everywhere! It pours from open city windows, gets drummed up on village corners, and is clapped and sung in every school. Senegalese music is so infectious that it is played all over the world. American musicians who invented hip-hop and rap were heavily influenced by it. And so were jazz, blues, and rock-and-roll musicians.

* Enslaved Senegalese people brought hundreds of their words to America—*guy* and *banana* are thought to come from Senegalese languages. Even the word *okay* may have come from the Senegalese language Wolof.

◉ Serigne Mactar Bâ is a Senegalese inventor. His most famous invention is an advanced weapons rocket.

Sierra Leone

In Sierra Leone, there are glass skyscrapers, marble mansions, concrete apartments, and houses made of cardboard boxes and corrugated iron. There are people who own expensive cars and people who do not even own shoes. There are families who fly abroad for vacations, and families who have to work every day of the year (including their children, who work in farms or factories or collecting trash on the streets for recycling).

★ Sierra Leone is one of the top ten diamond-producing countries in the world—but it's not a good idea to buy diamonds from there. Diamond mining is dangerous work, often done by children forced into working by soldiers.

Togo

Food is sold on every street corner in Togo. Corn is roasted on little fires, and spicy chicken is grilled on sticks for people to buy. In roadside stores, customers eat peanut stew, fried yams, and shrimp at rickety plastic tables. Old men sit under trees and buy the kola nuts they love so much from girls carrying them in baskets on their heads.

@ African food is popular around the world. Africans brought okra and black-eyed peas to America and taught the Europeans there how to grow rice.

✷ People all over West Africa love to chew kola nuts. They have more caffeine than coffee beans and were one of the original ingredients in Coca-Cola!

Central Africa

Burundi, Cameroon, Central African Republic, Chad, Democratic Republic of the Congo, Equatorial Guinea, Gabon, Republic of the Congo, and **São Tomé and Príncipe**

The second-biggest rain forest in the world covers Central Africa. It is loud with monkeys, parrots, and trillions of insects. But it might not be there for long. The rain forest people were the first people to live in Central Africa. They lived singing in the forest and hunting with spears and arrows. Then came those whose lifestyles now threaten the rain forest: tall farmers from West Africa who cleared the forests for their fields, nomadic herders from East Africa with cattle and goats that eat young trees, and Europeans greedy for oil, timber, minerals, and crops. Some Central Africans have kept traditional lifestyles, and others have chosen modern lives, but whether they are billionaires or beggars, bankers or farmers, oil rig workers or hunters, they all call Central Africa home!

Welcome to Central Africa!

"Nzoni gango" (Shango), "Bem-vindo!" (Portuguese),
"Boyei bolamu!" (Lingala), "Mbote!" (Kongo)

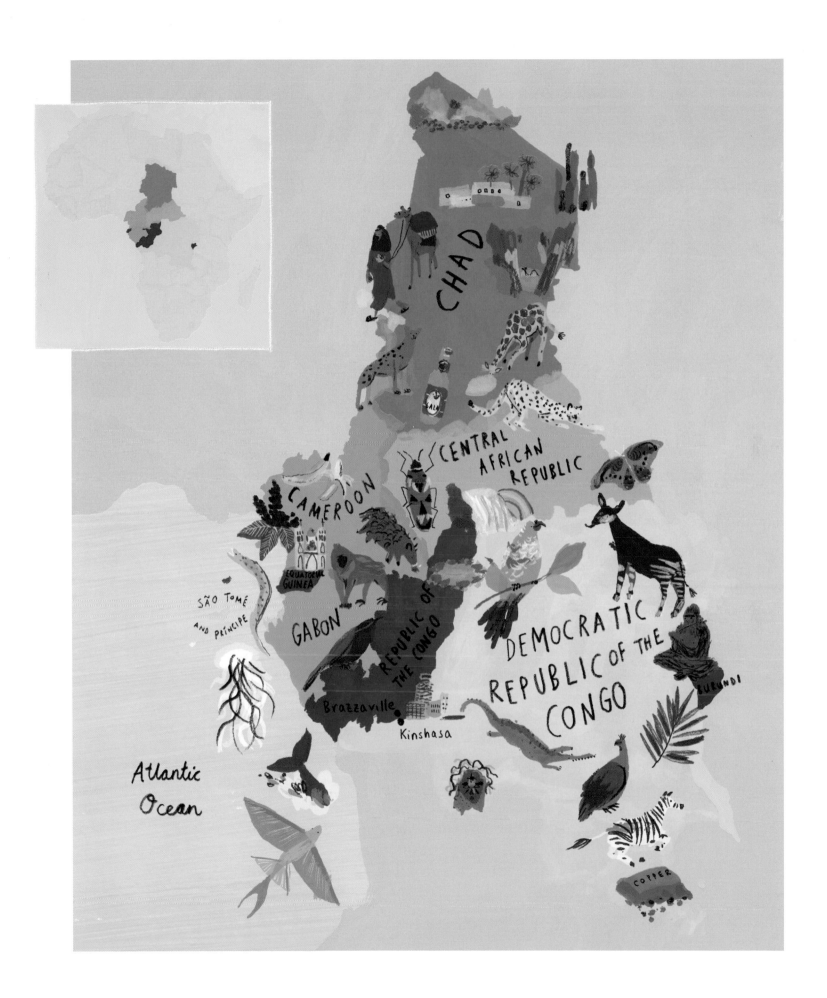

African Hairstyles

In Africa, most people's hair is very thick and very, very curly. It can get into impossible tangles. For this reason, lots of women wear their hair in the most amazing braids.

On special occasions (and on bad-hair days) in lots of African countries, women wear elaborate and eye-catching head scarves.

In some African countries, women wear hijabs. In others, men cover their heads and sometimes their faces, too.

Burundi

In Burundi, boys are taught to play huge drums by their fathers. It takes years and years of practice to be a drummer. You have to be able to dance, do acrobatics, and march balancing a huge drum on your head—while drumming wildly at the same time! The rhythms of Burundi drumming are powerful enough to make the whole world want to dance!

◉ Drums in Burundi are made from a tree that grows nowhere else in the world: the umuvugangoma tree.

✱ The Royal Drummers of Burundi are powerful, earsplitting, and awesome. Go online and hear for yourself!

Cameroon

In Cameroon, as all over Africa, some children are driven to school by their parents and play computer games when they get home. Other children have to walk to school no matter how far it is. Some of them wake at four a.m. and walk a long way to school, creeping past wild animals. Afterward, they work in the fields before doing their homework, and they don't have any devices to play on. But no matter how hard it is, children in Cameroon are determined to go to school. They want the chance to become engineers, doctors, lawyers, teachers, and scientists.

* Cameroon grows food that kids all over the world love—bananas, peanuts, sugar, and cocoa for chocolate. The people who grow these foods are often very poor because they are not paid enough for their work.

Sometimes they can't even afford to eat the things they grow for us! If you buy food that is labeled "fair trade" then you know the farmers have been paid fairly for their hard work.

Central African Republic

The Central African Republic is hundreds of miles from the sea on a huge high plateau covered with grassy savannas and thick forests. Through the forests, millions of butterflies flutter like flowery jewels. Over the savanna, the skies are lit with stars as big and bright as diamonds. And under the Central African Republic's soil lies more treasure: gold, uranium, oil, and diamonds.

⊚ There are more than six hundred species of butterflies in the Central African Republic.

✳ The needle in a normal magnetic compass points north nearly everywhere on Earth.

But don't get lost in the Central African Republic—the magnetic field under the ground there is unusually strong, which makes the needles in compasses go haywire.

Chad

Most people in Chad speak two, three, four, or five languages. More than 120 languages in total are spoken there, so no one can speak them all! To make sure people can understand one another, there are two official languages that everyone learns: Arabic and French. But people in Chad don't speak them exactly the way they're spoken in the rest of the world—they have their own Chadian versions. Language is like nature—it evolves.

● Chad is named after its biggest lake: Lake Chad. One thousand years ago, it was the biggest lake in the world. It is now far smaller and shrinking because of climate change. But dust from the dried-up lake still blows across the Atlantic, all the way to South America.

Democratic Republic of the Congo

There are so many rivers in the Democratic Republic of the Congo that it is easier and quicker to get around by boat than by car. Children paddle to school in canoes. Businesspeople go to work in speedboats. And everyone goes to visit family and friends using the ferries that steam up and down the Congo River— sometimes on trips that can take weeks and weeks and weeks. People sleep and cook and even shop on board. Just watch out for crocodiles!

✷ There are huge mines of the minerals casserite and coltan in the Democratic Republic of the Congo. Casserite is used to make cell phones and other handheld devices.

★ There are some weird and wonderful animals in the Congo. The okapi looks like a cross between a giraffe and a horse; its tongue is 18 inches (45 centimeters) long.

Equatorial Guinea

In Equatorial Guinea, it can rain for months and months and months. Then comes the dry season, when it won't rain for months and months and months. The sun gets hotter, the rivers dry up, and the ground turns to dust. When the rainy season comes back, children dance in the warm, fat, splashing raindrops. Everybody is glad that the grass and fields will turn green again . . . except people whose cars get stuck in the mud!

✳ Equatorial Guinea has both mainland and islands. When it is the rainy season on the mainland, the islands are usually dry. And when it is the rainy season on the islands, the mainland is usually dry.

⦿ Equatorial Guinea makes its money from oil, which is sold all over the world to create gasoline and plastic.

Gabon

In Gabon, the dark rain forest stretches right down to the beaches of the wild Atlantic Ocean. And there, both forest animals and ocean animals come out to play. Sea turtles wander in the shade of the trees and lay their eggs in the sand. Elephants splash with their babies in the shallows. And hippos surf the waves.

★ The government in Gabon is working hard to protect all its wonderful animals—even its oceans are a national park! Poachers only kill animals because it earns them good money. If people stop buying ivory, then poachers will stop killing elephants.

Republic of the Congo

Lake Tele in the Congo is where the Mokele-Mbembe lives. You haven't heard of the Mokele-Mbembe? It's as big as a dinosaur and as scary as a monster, and it hides in the lake like a crocodile. You don't believe me? Oh, well, not everybody believes in the Mokele-Mbembe. And not everybody believes in its cousin the Loch Ness monster in Scotland, either!

● Some African tales are more than 60,000 years old! The fact that they have never been forgotten even though they are not written down shows what brilliant stories they are.

✱ The capital city of the Congo, Brazzaville, is just across the river from the capital of the Democratic Republic of the Congo, Kinshasa. They're talked about like two sisters in a story, one friendly and beautiful, the other dangerous and scary. But which is which?

São Tomé and Príncipe

São Tomé and Príncipe is a country made up of two islands and four islets in the Atlantic Ocean. Rain forests cover the islands' mountains, turning them emerald green. Fishermen drop their nets into crystal-clear blue water. Tourists lie on the white sandy beaches. And farmers grow cocoa—to make the chocolate and sweet things we love to eat so much.

★ São Tomé and Príncipe grows a lot of the cocoa in the world. Cocoa beans are not only used to make chocolate. They are used to make beauty products, too.

North Africa

Algeria, Egypt, Libya, Mauritania, Morocco, Tunisia, and Western Sahara

North Africa is desert country, and the desert is called the Sahara. The Sahara is harder to cross than the Mediterranean Sea. This means that North African customs and traditions have more in common with those in the Middle East and Europe than with those in the rest of Africa. That's because for millennia, the Middle East and Europe were easier to get to!

The Romans, Greeks, and Turks all conquered North Africa and made it part of their empires. And then Morocco conquered southern Europe and made it part of its huge North African empire.

The few North Africans who did manage to cross the Sahara before the days of planes were nomadic Berber merchants, the original North African

people, with their long lines of camels carrying salt and gold. Wherever they stopped, people came to buy and sell goods. Those trading places became huge markets, and those markets became the great North African cities of today. You can still buy anything at those markets, from a computer chip to a fossil the size of a car. In fact, it is said that if you cannot buy something in the markets of North Africa, then you cannot buy it anywhere in the world!

Welcome to North Africa!

"AhLaN wa SahLaN!"
(Arabic)

"Amrehba sisswene"
(Berber)

"Bienvenue!"
(French)

Football Is Best

The African continent is wild about football, the sport known as soccer in the United States. Football was played in Africa long before the international rules of the game were decided in 1860.

Some people in Africa like wrestling or boxing, other people like canoeing or basketball, some are fans of cricket or rugby, but everybody is wild about football.

The weather is mostly warm enough to play outside all year round. And most children don't have expensive toys and gadgets to distract them from playing footie. Rich kids wear expensive sneakers while poor kids wear rags, but in this beautiful game only speed and skill count.

The Africa Cup of Nations—the biggest tournament in Africa—is held every two years. So far, Egypt has won it more times than any other country. People all over Africa follow the tournament, but they follow other leagues, too. Everyone has their favorite European clubs, a lot of whose best players are African!

Algeria

In Algeria, women work everywhere—in shops, schools, offices, businesses, hospitals, courts, and mosques. More than half of all university students are women. And many doctors, scientists, lawyers, and judges are women, too.

Cave paintings in the Algerian desert show people hunting the herds of animals that lived there thousands of years ago, when the Sahara was lush, rich savanna. But now most people live on the coast—where the climate is just like California's—because the rest of the country is either snowy mountains or scorching desert.

● Geographically, Algeria is the largest country in Africa.

✳ Soon Algeria will have one of the biggest solar energy farms in the world.

Egypt

Egypt is probably the most well-known African country. Tourists love visiting its famous pyramids and taking boat rides down the magnificent Nile River, where the biggest crocodiles in Africa live. The river runs through the capital city of Cairo. It's a gigantic city with one of the best universities, and the strongest army, in the whole of Africa.

★ Egypt is the largest Arab country in the world and is on two continents: Africa and Asia.

◉ Because most of Egypt is desert, 99 percent of Egyptian people live in only 3 percent of the country—along the edges of the Nile River. Without this wide river, which brings rich soil as well as water, Egypt would never have become a great nation.

Libya

The Libyan Desert, which is part of the Sahara, is one of the hottest and driest in the world. Sometimes ten, twenty, or even thirty years go by without rain! Even the Berbers and the desert-loving Bedouins will not go into parts of it. They prefer their beautiful cities, built around oases. The most beautiful Berber city is Ghadames, "Pearl of the Desert." Once, only men walked its winding streets, while women visited one another in their connected roof gardens. Now men and women walk together in Libyan cities and sit together in cafés, drinking coffee and laughing with their children.

✳ Along the Libyan coast are the ruins of an ancient Greek temple to Zeus at Cyrene, as well as the ruins of a Roman city called Leptis Magna, which was home to the Roman emperor Septimius Severus and was nearly as important as Rome.

✳ Cyrene was also home to one of the oldest Jewish communities in the world, dating back to 300 BCE.

Mauritania

Mauritania stretches deep into the Sahara desert and down into land called the Sahel. *Sahel* means "shoreline" in Arabic. The Sahel is the southern shoreline of the Sahara, a desert as wide as an ocean. It is dry and dusty, with thorny trees and prickly bushes and spiky grasses. Luckily, Mauritania is full of oases, too, where springs of clean water bubble up from the dry ground and where trees, farms, and whole towns can grow.

★ The desert is growing, and towns and villages are being buried under sand. The people who lived there are escaping to the capital city on the coast. Others are fighting climate change.

✳ There is still slavery in Mauritania: actual people are bought and sold and forced to work for free. They have no rights and no choices. Lots of people are fighting to change this.

Morocco

In the heart of every North African city is a medina—the old town. In the heart of the medina is the souk—the ancient market where the traders who crisscrossed the Sahara on camelback sold their goods. The medina in the Moroccan city of Marrakesh is surrounded by 12 miles (19 kilometers) of rosy-pink walls. Spices, carpets, leather, gold, olives, and hundreds of other things are for sale in its souk district, just as they have been for thousands of years. And now there are watches, phones, and cameras, too.

● Medinas all have narrow and winding mazelike streets. The streets are narrow to keep out the scorching desert sun. They are winding to keep out the sands of sandstorms that can bury cities. And they are mazelike to confuse enemy raiders!

✱ Several international car companies have factories in Morocco.

Tunisia

In Tunisia, beautiful golden-domed mosques, high spiky cathedrals, and cool tiled synagogues—where Muslim and Christian and Jewish people go to pray—crowd together. Along the shady streets, families sit in restaurants and cafés, eating their favorite foods. Some prefer fast food, while others enjoy traditional stews served with couscous and flatbread—but everyone loves to drink Tunisia's super-sweet mint tea!

● Stews called tagines are cooked all over North Africa in thick pottery dishes with cone lids. The dishes are called tagines, too! The stew is made by putting meat or chickpeas in the bottom of the pot and sprinkling them with spices. Vegetables are piled in a pyramid shape on top, and the dish is covered and cooked in the red-hot embers of a fire.

✤ Tunisia sells more olives than almost anywhere else in the world. Lots of people have jobs looking after olive trees and harvesting the olives. Other people work in the many, many factories in Tunisia that make clothes and shoes and car parts and electronic machinery.

Western Sahara

Western Sahara is where the Sahrawi people live. They call their country the Sahrawi Arab Democratic Republic. The Moroccan government took over Western Sahara in 1975, saying it was part of Morocco. The Sahrawi people are still fighting against this—they want to rule themselves. Once, the Sahrawi men roamed with their herds, looking for grass, while the women stayed at home in charge of the families, the finances, and the law. Now most Sahrawi people live in refugee camps, waiting for the war to end.

☆ The Sahrawi people love to drink green tea. They say the first cup is bitter, like life. The second cup is gentle, like death. And the third cup is sweet, like love.

★ The Sahara International Film Festival is held in Western Sahara every year. It is the only film festival in the world that takes place in a refugee camp.

Index

Find Out More

More facts and figures: **factmonster.com/countries**

More about African languages: **omniglot.com**

More about African music: **worldmusic.net/guide/**

More about African geography: **dkfindout.com/us/earth/continents/Africa** and
nationalgeographic.org/encyclopedia/africa-physical-geography

More about African wildlife: **awf.org**
and the David Attenborough documentary *Africa* (BBC, 2013)

For animated cartoons set in Africa: **binoandfino.com**

And for stories set in Africa: **booksfortopics.com/africa**